The Thomas KIDDOS,
Big + Little!
with love + thanks!
we hope that
you enjoy Scooter!

♥ Wilson & Scooter

I am Scooter
the invincible horse

A book for all the freedom-loving
creatures of the world

By Wilson Farrar

Illustrations by Jensen Tan

Permission requests for educational or textbook use should be addressed to Wilson@SuperScooter.Me

SuperScooter is a Registered Trademark

ISBN # 978-0-9909735-0-8

Printed in the United States of America

FIRST EDITION

Written by Wilson Farrar

Illustrations by Jensen Tan

Book design by Schaub&Company, Inc.

www.schaubco.com

For additional books please go to www.SuperScooter.Me

Books are available in quantity for promotional or premium use.

Please email SpecialSales@SuperScooter.Me for Information on discounts and terms.

Scooter Says, "I am dedicated to inspiring the hearts and minds of future generations to pursue their dreams and cherish the liberty that makes it all possible!"

This book is dedicated to you!

Super **JENNIFER & JASON** ✱

AND **LILLY, ELYSE**

AND **MACKALL**

✱ THANK YOU FOR YOUR SERVICE! ✱

Hello!

Hello, I am Scooter. My friends call me "SuperScooter." I am actually a small horse, but I have a big heart and great determination and because of this I have lived a very long time, overcoming great obstacles, and achieving wonderful things.

I am old now, and very happy. I've learned a lot in my life and I am grateful for many things. My gift to you is to share what I've learned so that you too can have an amazing life full of experiences that will make your spirit soar and your heart sing!

I will show you how!

Scooter says,

"You have
the power within you
to do whatever you want."

Scooter says,

"Never compare yourself
to other people,
only to yourself."

Scooter says,

"Being happy is more fun
than being sad.
So be happy!"

Scooter says,

"Smile at people every day,
and your world will be a nicer,
happier place."

Scooter says,

"Create beauty
in your life."

Scooter says,

"Get out in nature
and enjoy!"

Scooter says,

"Take time to be quiet."

Scooter says,

"Figure out what is most important and then do that first."

Scooter says,

"Do what makes your spirit soar
and your heart sing."

Scooter says,

"Move your body.
It feels good
and is good for you."

Scooter says,

"Being clean inside and out
makes you happy."

Scooter says,

"Remember to
pamper yourself."

Scooter says,

"Naps are important."

Scooter says,

"You program yourself with your thoughts, so program yourself with positive thoughts."

Scooter says,

"Happiness
comes from within."

Scooter says,

"Show everyone you love
that you love them."

Scooter says,

"Be kind to animals."

Scooter says,

"Make someone happy."

Scooter says,

"Embrace all
religions and philosophies
based in kindness."

Scooter says,

"Friends are the family
that you choose."

Scooter says,

"You always have time
to call your family."

Scooter says,

"If you remember that you don't know everything, you will be much more interested and much more interesting."

Scooter says,

"Study The Greats."

Scooter says,

"Pursue the truth
in all things."

Scooter says,

"Choices matter.
Choose wisely."

Scooter says,

"Freedom of speech
lives here.
Cherish it!"

Scooter says,

"The freedom to succeed
makes America great.
Do your best!"

Scooter says,

"Follow your heart."

Scooter says,

"Above all else,
be true to yourself."

Scooter says,

"Make your dreams come true!"

Scooter says,

"Remember,
Anything is possible!"

Scooter is a 30 year old Peruvian Paso, who was born "Espiritu Amable del Inca" (friendly spirit of the Incas) in San Jose, California on April 28, 1984. His mother, "Jubileo" was from Peru, and his father, "Cerrazon" was born in the United States.

Scooter grew up in the hills of Saratoga, California where he enjoyed roaming freely in the wide-open spaces, eating from fresh pear and fig trees, and playing with his horsey friends. In addition to being a smooth, gaited, fast and spirited ride, Scooter was a parade and show horse, winning numerous ribbons, and demonstrating to enthusiastic fans what it means to "have heart."

I met Scooter in 2003 after he had retired from his show days. We became fast friends, exploring the tall grass and trees, taking note of rabbits, deer and coyotes, and enjoying time in the fields together. I have always admired Scooter's great spirit, kind soul, fearless attitude, sense of humor, and gentle demeanor toward babies, bunny rabbits, dogs and all living creatures. I have learned a lot from him. He is a courageous being who perseveres no matter what.

Over the years, Scooter has hosted friends from around the world including people from Australia, Bangladesh, Brazil, Canada, China, Denmark, Ecuador, England, Germany, Ghana, Guatemala, Honduras, Hungary, India, Iran, Ireland, Israel, Italy, Malaysia, Mexico, Nicaragua, Pakistan, Russia, Singapore, South Africa, Spain, Sweden, Turkey, Ukraine and all over the USA, many of whom have attended his birthday parties. Those who meet him delight in his friendly character and his interest in visitors, especially when they have a little carrot for him.

Happy thoughts to you! You make the world a nicer place!

Scooter and Wilson, Saratoga, California

65

The end?

Scooter in Saratoga, California